*This book belongs to*

Sophie Annie

Campbell

*A gift on the occasion of*

Your Christening

*with love from*

Great Granny Olphert

(Pokie)

*Date*

22 | 9 | 2019

# Christening
# Prayers

Compiled and written by
Sally Ann Wright
Illustrated by
Honor Ayres

'Children are a
blessing and a gift
from the Lord.'

Psalm 127:3

# About me

My name is ..................................................................................

..................................................................................

I was born on ............................................................................

I weighed ..................................................................................

My eyes are ...............................................................................

My hair is .................................................................................

I live at this address ...................................................................

..................................................................................

..................................................................................

..................................................................................

My grandfather's name

......................................

Date and place of birth

......................................

......................................

My grandmother's name

......................................

Date and place of birth

......................................

......................................

My father's name

......................................

My father's date and place of birth

......................................

......................................

My name

......................................

......................................

My grandfather's name
.............................................
Date and place of birth
.............................................
.............................................

My grandmother's name
.............................................
Date and place of birth
.............................................
.............................................

My mother's name
.............................................
My mother's date and place of birth
.............................................
.............................................

# My family

# My progress

Lord, bless us and protect us.
Lord, smile on us and show us your love.
Lord, help us and take care of us.
Lord, guide us, keep us and grant us your peace.

*I first smiled* ...................................................................................

*I cut my first tooth* .........................................................................

*I first sat up* ..................................................................

*I first crawled* ..................................................................

*My first words* ..................................................................

..................................................................

*I first walked* ..................................................................

*My favourite things* ..................................................

..................................................................

..................................................................

# On being a parent

Lord God, our creator,
you made us all
and you made us like yourself,
able to love and be loved,
to share and enjoy the wonderful world you have made.
Thank you now for the wonder of this new life,
the gift of this child.

Thank you that you know us by name
and have cared about us since before we were born.
Help us as we learn
the joys and challenges of parenthood,
to live one day at a time
and to trust you to provide for us
as each new need arises.

# The gift of a child

Lord, you are the giver of all good things.
Thank you for this precious gift,
a child to love and nurture,
to care for and to protect.

We pray for your love to live in us
so that we may be able to guide
with wisdom, discipline with love,
and teach by our good example.
May we be encouraging and affirming
so that our child may grow up to be whole,
to be the person you intended from the beginning.

# The mystery of love

Thank you, God,
for the wonder of life
and the mystery of human love.
Thank you for the capacity
to share love with one another,
and to open our lives to this child.
Let your love fill us
and spill over in blessing
so that all our lives may be enriched.

19

# Guard and guide

Father God,
may this child learn to love all that is true,
grow in wisdom and strength
and, in due time, come to know you
as creator, guide and friend.

◆

Almighty God,
you are Lord of the universe,
and all love and strength come from you.
Bless us now so that we can nurture
the precious gift of this child
and bring us joy in this new creation.

# Thank you, God

Butterflies thank you for wings to fly,
fish give thanks for the sea.
Birds give thanks with the songs they sing,
but I thank you for making me me!

———◆———

Thank you, God, for making me ME.
Thank you for eyes that see your world,
for ears that hear the things you have made,
a nose so I can smell my dinner cooking
and a mouth to praise you!
Thank you for fingers and toes
and for loving me, just the way I am.
In the name of the Father, and of the Son,
and of the Holy Spirit.

# Prayers for today

Thank you, Lord, that you are here with me,
that your love surrounds me,
and the gift of a new day is before me.

Thank you, Lord Jesus,
for my home and family,
for food to eat and a warm bed
to sleep in at night.
Please look after children
who have none of these things
and keep them safe tonight.

Thank you for the world so sweet,
thank you for the food we eat,
thank you for the birds that sing,
thank you, God, for everything.

# I am special

Thank you, Father God,
that you made me and I am special to you.
Thank you that you know all about me.
You know when I wake up and when I go to sleep.
You know when I am at home and when I go out.
You know when I am sad and when I am happy.
You know when I am lonely
or when I have lots of friends.
You know when I am cross or grumpy
and when I am kind to other people.
Thank you that you know me
and you still love me, just as I am.
Thank you, Father God,
that you made me
and that I am special to you.
Thank you for loving me, just as I am.

27

# Thank you
# for the world

For woods and fields,
for sea and sky,
for flowers, trees,
family and friends,
all the creatures around me,
and all your gifts,
thank you, God!

28

Creator God,
thank you for all the animals you have made.
Thank you for furry cats and playful dogs,
for hamsters in wheels and long-eared rabbits.
Help us to look after them well
as part of the world you have made.

Spotty ladybirds, stripy snails,
tiny spiders, buzzing bees,
slimy slugs with silvery trails,
wiggly worms and centipedes,
crawling creatures with long tails:
Thank you, God,
you made all these.

# Family and friends

Please God, look after everyone in my family.
Whether at home or far away,
keep them safe and well today.

Bless our home, dear Lord.
Teach us to love one another,
support and help one another,
and forgive one another,
as you forgive us.

# God is great!

Praise God, from whom all blessings flow;
praise him, all creatures here below;
praise him above, you heavenly host;
praise Father, Son, and Holy Ghost.

*Bishop Thomas Ken*

O Lord God,
how great you are!
When I look at the sky,
and the moon and the stars,
I feel so tiny,
I don't understand why you care about me.
O Lord God, how great you are!

*Adapted from Psalm 8*

Lord God,
you are great and wonderful
and you made the whole wide world!
You are kind and good,
marvellous and mighty,
ever living, ever loving,
everlasting, everywhere.

*Jan Godfrey*

# Day by day

Thank you for sleep
and bringing us safely through another night.
Thank you for a new morning
and for health and strength.
Lord, be with us throughout this day
as we eat and work and play.
Fill us with your love
for everything and everyone around us.

Jesus, Friend of little children,
Father God, be a friend to me;
take my hand, and ever keep me
close to thee.

*Walter J Matham*

# Sorry

Father God,
I am sorry when I say things that are unkind.
I am sorry when I do things that make other people sad.
Please help me to say sorry to them
and to be kinder tomorrow.

You know what I was like today, Lord.
I was angry
I was selfish
I was greedy
I was proud
I was unkind
I was unhelpful.
I am sorry.

# Please help

I want to be generous, Lord,
but sometimes it's hard to share.
I want to be kind, Lord,
but sometimes I am mean.
I want to say the right thing,
but sometimes the wrong thing comes out.
I need your help, Lord,
to be generous and kind and loving.
Please help me.

I am sorry, Lord,
because today
I didn't listen
I didn't see
I didn't speak kindly
I didn't help
I didn't make peace
I didn't forgive
I didn't love.
I am sorry, Lord.

# When I am worried

Come close to me, Lord,
and hear my prayer.
Answer me,
because I need your help.
Look after me,
because I love you.
Help me,
because I trust you and you are my God.

Lord Jesus,
you told us not be worried about anything,
but I am worried about tomorrow.
Help me to tell you about my worries
and then to trust you to help me.

# When someone dies

I don't want to say goodbye, Lord.
I am not ready.
I don't want things to change, Lord.
I am not ready.
Help me to be happy with what is past,
make me brave to face today,
and give me faith to face the future.

———◆———

Lord, you said there are many rooms in God's house.
Please make a special room ready for me,
and all the people in my family
and all those I love,
when it is our turn to die.

# Help me to be kind

O God, help me never to judge another person
until I have walked two weeks in his shoes.

---

Lord, please give me
hands that are quick to give and slow to take,
feet that go where you want me to be,
eyes that see the best in everyone,
ears that hear only good things,
a voice that speaks the truth kindly,
and a loving, forgiving heart.

---

Lord, let me not judge others
by what I see or hear,
without knowing,
or understanding,
anything about them.

# Sharing and caring

Father God,
help me not to want more things than I need,
help me not to judge other people by what they have,
and help me to share everything you have given me.

Lord, you have given me so many good things.
Sometimes I forget how lucky I am.
Help me to remember,
and to share with other people.

# Graces

For every cup and plateful
Lord, make us truly grateful.

---

O God, your generous love surrounds us,
and everything we enjoy
comes from you.

For what we are about to receive,
may the Lord make us truly thankful;
through Jesus Christ our Lord.

Yours Lord, are the greatness, the power,
the glory and the majesty,
for everything we have comes from you.

For this and all his many mercies,
God's holy name be blessed and praised;
through Christ our Lord.

# Prayers for others

Lord Jesus, you are the Good Shepherd.
You look after me, and care for me.
Lord Jesus, Good Shepherd,
look after my family and friends today.

Loving Father,
please look after all who are not well.
Comfort those who are in pain,
or who are worried or sad.
Give peace to those who are old or frightened.
Help us to be loving and helpful to our families,
kind to everyone we know,
and generous to anyone who needs our help.

# One world

Loving Father, creator of all people,
you love everyone you have made:
different ages and different sizes,
different shapes and different colours.
Help us to learn from one another,
share with one another,
and love one another.

———◆———

Help me, Lord, to love my family.
Help my family to love the people they meet.
Help us all to love those in other countries.
Help all countries of the world
to love each other and live together in peace.
Lord, let it start here with me.

# When things go wrong

Heavenly Father,
we pray for peace in your world.
Where people fight, take away their hate;
where people hate, fill them with love;
where people suffer, bring them your peace;
where people mourn, give them comfort and hope.
Heavenly Father,
we pray for peace in your world.

Help your world, Father God,
because people are suffering.
Some have lost their homes;
some have lost their families;
some people are starving;
some are surrounded by fighting;
others are in pain or dying.
Please comfort and help each one,
and help us to share our money,
our food, our love, our prayers,
to help them in their need.

# Birthday prayer

Today it's my birthday!
I am one year older
and there are lots of surprises!
Thank you, Father God,
for cards and a cake,
for presents and a party.
Thank you most of all
for all my family and friends
who love me and care for me
and will make today
a special day.

# Christmas prayers

Dear Father God,
thank you for Christmas.
Thank you for the gift of Jesus
to be our friend, our Saviour and our king.

⟶ ◆ ⟵

May the joy of the angels,
the wonder of the shepherds,
and the peace of Jesus Christ,
fill our hearts this Christmas time.

⟶ ◆ ⟵

Father God, may we this Christmas time:
make room for you with the innkeeper,
sing with the angels,
rejoice with the shepherds,
seek you with the wise men
and worship you as Lord and King.

# New year prayer

May this new year
be a new beginning for our family.
We cannot see what things,
good or bad, lie ahead of us.
Help us to thank you for the good things,
trust you if things are hard for us,
and ask for your help whatever happens.
At the beginning of this new year, Lord,
hear our prayer.

# Easter prayers

Thank you, Lord Jesus,
that the sadness of your cruel death
on Good Friday has a happy ending.
Thank you, Lord Jesus,
that you died so my sin could be forgiven.
Thank you, Lord Jesus,
that you rose from the dead
so that I can one day live with you in Heaven.
Thank you, Lord Jesus!

⸺ ◆ ⸺

Dear Father God,
Jesus became a servant to teach us how to love,
and died on a cross so that we might live.
Teach me to put other people first
and to think about their needs before my own.

# Harvest prayers

May God
who clothes the lilies of the field,
and feeds the birds of the sky,
who leads the lambs to pasture
and guides the deer to water,
clothe us, feed us, lead us and guide us,
and change us to be more like
our loving Creator.

All good gifts around us
are sent from heaven above.
Then thank the Lord,
oh thank the Lord,
for all his love.

*Matthias Claudius*

# Holiday prayers

For salty sea and sunny skies,
for walks in mountains and hillsides,
for time to rest and time to play,
thank you, God, for holidays.

Splashy sea,
big blue sky,
shiny stones,
grasses tall.
Trickling sand,
knobbly shells...
Thank you, God!
You made it all.

For the sun in the sky
and the wind in the trees,
for rivers, streams and mountaintops,
for open spaces and time to play,
for friends and family
and all the good things we can enjoy,
thank you, Lord.

# A traveller's blessing

God the Father, please keep us in your care;
Lord Jesus, be our constant friend;
Holy Spirit, guide us in all we do.
Bless us and protect us
until we come safely
to the end of our journey.

# The Lord's Prayer

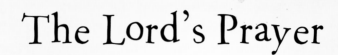

Our Father in heaven,
hallowed be your name.
Your Kingdom come,
your will be done,
on earth as in heaven.
Give us today our daily bread.

Forgive us our sins,
as we forgive those
who sin against us.
Lead us not into temptation,
but deliver us from evil.
For the kingdom,
the power
and the glory are yours,
now and for ever.
Amen

# St Patrick's Breastplate

Christ be with me, Christ within me,
Christ behind me, Christ before me,
Christ beside me, Christ to win me,

Christ to comfort and restore me,
Christ beneath me, Christ above me,
Christ in quiet, Christ in danger,
Christ in hearts of all that love me,
Christ in mouth of friend and stranger.

# The prayer of St Francis

Lord, make us instruments of your peace.
Where there is hatred, let us sow love;
where there is injury, let there be pardon;
where there is discord, union;
where there is doubt, faith;
where there is despair, hope;
where there is darkness, light;
where there is sadness, joy;
for your mercy
and for your truth's sake.

# The prayer of Richard of Chichester

Lord Jesus Christ, we thank you
for all the benefits you have won for us,
for all the pains and insults you have borne for us.
Most merciful redeemer,
friend and brother,
may we know you more clearly,
love you more dearly,
and follow you more nearly,
day by day.

# The prayer of Ignatius of Loyola

Teach us, good Lord,
to serve you as you deserve;
to give and not to count the cost;
to fight and not to heed the wounds;
to toil and not to seek for rest;
to labour and not to seek for any reward,
save that of knowing that we do your will.

# The prayer of St Teresa of Avila

Christ has no body now on earth but ours,
no hands but ours, no feet but ours.
Ours are the eyes through which must look out
Christ's compassion on the world.
Ours are the feet
with which he is to go about doing good.
Ours are the hands
with which he is to bless all people now.
So Lord, give us able bodies,
eyes to see the need around us,
willing hands and feet, to serve you now.

# The Sarum Primer

God be in my head, and in my understanding;
God be in my eyes, and in my looking;
God be in my mouth, and in my speaking;
God be in my heart, and in my thinking;
God be at mine end, and at my departing.

# Bedtime prayers

Bring light into the darkness, Lord,
and guard us, guide us
and keep us safe from danger
this night and always.

Into your loving care,
into your keeping,
you who are everywhere,
take us, we pray.

* * *

Into your hands, Lord,
I commit myself tonight.
Let angels surround my bed,
and peaceful thoughts
be always in my head.

* * *

Angel of God, my guardian dear,
to whom God's love commits me here,
every night be at my side,
to light and guard
to rule and guide.

# God's peace

May the peace of God,
which passes all understanding,
keep our hearts and minds
in the knowledge and love of God,
and of his Son Jesus Christ our Lord;
and the blessing of God almighty,
the Father, the Son, and the Holy Spirit,
be with us and remain with us always.

# An Irish blessing

At the first light of sun:
God bless you.
When the long day is done:
God bless you.
In your smiles and in your tears:
God bless you.
Through each day of your years:
God bless you.

# Blessings

God bless all those that I love;
God bless all those that love me;
God bless all those that love those that I love
and all those that love those that love me.

May the Lord bless us and watch over us.
May the Lord make his face shine upon us
and be gracious to us,
may the Lord look kindly on us
and give us peace;
and the blessing of God almighty,
the Father, the Son, and the Holy Spirit,
be with us and remain with us now and every day.

*Based on Numbers 6:24-26*

# Index

**PALM TREE**

Buxhall, Stowmarket, Suffolk IP14 3BW
Tel: +44 (0) 1449 737978  E-mail: info@kevinmayhew.com  www.Kevinmayhew.com

Product Code: 1600007. ISBN: 978 1 83858 007 0

First edition 2016.
This edition 2019

Publishing Director Annette Reynolds
Art Director Gerald Rogers
Pre-production Doug Hewitt

Printed and bound in Malaysia